Copyright ©1989 by Paul Stickland. All rights reserved under International and Pan-American Copyright Conventions. Published in the United States by Random House, Inc., New York. Designed by Herman Lelie. Produced by Mathew Price Ltd., Old Rectory House, Marston Magna, Yeovil BA22 8DT, Somerset, England.

Library of Congress Cataloging-in-Publication Data: Stickland, Paul. Machines as big as monsters. SUMMARY: Text and pictures introduce large machines, such as a dump truck, various types of cranes, and spacecraft. 1. Machinery — Juvenile literature. [1. Machinery] I. Title. TJ147.S75 1989 621.8 88-26511 ISBN: 0-394-83913-7 (trade); 0-394-93913-1 (lib. bdg.)

Manufactured in Italy 1 2 3 4 5 6 7 8 9 0

MACHINES
AS BIG AS
MONSTERS

PAUL STICKLAND

Random House 🏠 New York

The Terex Titan is the largest dump truck in the world. It has a huge diesel engine that powers electric motors for each of its 10 wheels, and it can carry up to 350 tons at a time. This one is taking copper ore from the quarry to the factory.

This monstrous floating crane is lowering the platform of an oil rig precisely into place. The crane is positioned by two tugboats and also by its own propellers. Besides building rigs, it is also used for salvaging sunken ships.

A walking dragline excavator rumbles slowly along on caterpillar tracks. This one is digging out huge mouthfuls of sand in a bucket big enough to hold a bulldozer. It is cutting a canal through the desert to bring water to the dry lands.

This gantry crane is built to lift steel containers out of the ship's hold and onto the dock. It moves around on wheels, up and down the harbor edge, working all day and all night. It is operated by the man in the red cab.

These machines are demolishing old buildings so that new ones can be built in their place. One is crunching concrete beams in its steel jaws. Two others, looking like mechanical hens, are hydraulic hammers smashing rubble into smaller pieces.

How do you build a house on top of a mountain? The answer is you build it down in the valley and have this flying crane take it up. It can carry buildings of up to 10 tons and put them down in exactly the right place.

The Galaxy C5 is the largest aircraft in the world. When it is ready to load, it sinks down onto its 28 gigantic wheels, its nose comes up, and its ramp comes down just like a huge mouth opening. This one is loading 16 trucks, each weighing three quarters of a ton. When they are all inside and its giant mouth is shut, it will rise up off its wheels again and take off into the sky.

Skylab was the first space station to be lived in by astronauts. It circled the earth far out in space, where there is no air and no gravity.
Three teams of three men were brought up and back by rockets.

This bucket-wheel excavator swings around in a circle, scooping up minerals in buckets attached to a revolving wheel. Conveyor belts then take the minerals all the way to the factory. Even though it is as tall as a skyscraper, the excavator can move about on its caterpillar tracks.

The Thames River barrier is a dam built to protect London from surging tides. Freak storms could otherwise cause the river to flood and devastate the city. Each gate lies flat on the riverbed until it is needed. Then wheels at either end move it into the upright position. The red crosses and green arrows tell ships which gates are open.

The chain-bucket dredger is making a deep channel for ships to sail through. It scoops up soft sand and mud from the harbor floor and pours it into the barge standing by. The barge will then take the mud out to sea and dump it—or even make little islands out of it.

After a while any asphalt road wears out and must be repaired. First the road is broken up. Next this resurfacing machine comes and sucks the bits into its revolving oven. There they are melted down, and then the asphalt is spread back on the road, ready to be rolled flat.